Should I Sue?

Andrew Thelander

FIAT JUSTITIA RUAT CAELUM

Let Justice be done though the Heavens may fall.

CONTENTS

NOTICE

This book contains general advice but it does not contain *legal* advice. Every dispute is unique. If you have a legal problem, you should consult a practicing lawyer promptly. Your lawyer will ascertain the relevant facts of your case and advise you on the law of the relevant jurisdiction, something which is altogether beyond the scope of this little book.

1 INTRODUCTION

So you have a legal problem and everyone tells you to go see a lawyer. Is it wise to ask a lawyer the question: "Should I sue?" Isn't that a bit like asking a beautician "Do I need makeup?" or asking a fitness trainer "Should I lose some weight?" You'll get an answer for sure but will it be an impartial one? Will it be an answer that has you and your interests as its sole concern? I have found that many people don't trust lawyers to give truly disinterested advice about suing in court. *Lawyers make money from litigating. Why would they want to discourage people from going to court?* That's what nearly everyone thinks. Who can blame them? I don't – even though, in my experience, most lawyers are professional and feel themselves duty bound to advise against litigating when prospects of success are lacking. After all, lawyers want to be on the winning side in court, not the losing side. To be seen as "unsuccessful" harms their reputation.

The law of the land and the legal system, however, are rarely "black and white." There are lots of grey areas where different people have different legal rights that overlap and clash and nobody knows exactly how a court would untangle the legal mess that develops when both sides of a dispute insist on "enforcing their rights." Both sides usually come up with some good and persuasive arguments in their favour and the lawyers normally do a good job "selling" those arguments to the court. But at the end of the day, only one side can win. It's often "touch and go" as to who the winner will be. The losing lawyer – like the losing litigant – sincerely believed in the merits of his or her case and everyone was hopeful the court would agree.

However, if you are contemplating litigating in court, there is one BIG distinction you need to remember at all times. The litigation is YOURS and not your lawyer's. If your case loses miserably, your lawyer will be able to sit back and say: "I acted on my client's instructions." He will have copies of some long letters of advice he sent you full of "ifs, buts and maybes" about his advice on your dispute and how a winning result cannot be guaranteed. In short, as a client who gives the go-ahead for litigation, you have to remember that the litigation is your baby and you won't be able to hand it back to the hospital if it keeps you awake at night.

For most of us, deciding to sue is a BIG DECISION. It has cost implications: financial costs, time costs, emotional costs, social costs. It's one episode in your life when you really need to THINK CLEARLY. When you are embroiled in a legal dispute, however, it's a stressful time – often a time of crisis. Emotions are running high and the logical brain doesn't get the energy and time for reflection it needs to sort through thorny issues with clarity and wisdom. That's when some people descend into a state of emotional exhaustion and rely too much or too exclusively on their lawyer's advice or don't really connect with what their lawyer is telling them. They just hand the dispute over to their lawyer - "Fix it!" – and then try to wash their hands of the matter just like Pontius Pilate did.

This book will help you avoid that mistake. It will help you TAKE OWNERSHIP of your legal problem. It will help you THINK CLEARLY about the big issues that are often overlooked when people ask: "Should I sue?" There is no need to feel alone and confused. Humans have been litigating for THOUSANDS OF YEARS. There is a huge body of ethical thinking and philosophical wisdom on the subject of litigation. Confucius, the Buddha, Jesus – they all had something to say about whether or not you should sue! MAKE USE OF THAT WISDOM and ensure that the resolution of your legal problem – whether by litigation or some other means - doesn't DESTROY you, financially and emotionally, but STRENGHTENS AND ENRICHES you as a person.

2 TWO QUESTIONS, NOT ONE

So you have a legal problem and you've made an appointment to see a lawyer. That's good. But what are you going to ask him? Most people don't give much thought to this. They just bundle together all their paperwork, lug it into the lawyer's office and tell their story as coherently as they can manage, skipping a relevant point here and there to save time – because everyone knows lawyers' hourly rates are crippling! At the end of their summation, they bleat out three short words: "CAN I SUE?" Those words are the acorn that can grow into an oak tree. The question they form is multi-faceted and rich with potential implications. As a possible litigant, you owe it to yourself to UNDERSTAND your situation right from the start. Only then can you plan and make decisions about what is an appropriate solution for your problem.

Let's begin with the difference between the words 'can' and 'should.' In this context, they denote the difference between 'law' and 'ethics.' Just because something is legal doesn't necessarily mean it's ethical or the right thing to do. Legal academics usually quote an extreme example at this point: those famous laws passed by the Nazi government of Germany in the 1930s allowing the confiscation of property from German citizens of Jewish heritage. Okay, so kicking Jews out of their houses became perfectly legal … but it was still a completely immoral thing to do. You're probably not likely to face such a stark gap between law and ethics in your dispute today. But you won't escape the issue entirely. There's a good chance some people in your social network will query whether you're "doing the right thing." They might think you're being "litigious" or "greedy" or "hard" or "playing the victim." It's no answer to these allegations that you are "perfectly within your legal rights." These people are not disputing that you CAN sue; they are questioning whether you SHOULD sue. When you ask your lawyer "Can I sue?" and he replies "Yes," that may answer the legal question but it doesn't answer the ethical question. THERE ARE TWO BASIC QUESTIONS INVOLVED IN LITIGATION, NOT ONE. Because of his specialist training and experience, your lawyer is well placed to advise you on whether or not you have a good case at law. And you are PAYING for that specialist legal advice so make sure you listen to it carefully and understand it! But when it comes to the ethical question of whether or not you *should* sue, your lawyer is NOT an expert. You and he are on the same level. He may well have an opinion that he's willing to share – and, as someone who works in the court system for a living, why wouldn't he? – but you must always bear in mind that, on the question of what is right and wrong, you are just as much an expert as your lawyer. He may be more eloquent than you. He may be able to quote persuasive examples off the cuff to support his view. But your gut feeling and your thoughts on right and wrong are not inferior to his. And remember, if you go ahead and sue, it will be YOUR litigation and not his! It's therefore essential that you are satisfied IN YOURSELF that you are doing the right thing.

So you've taken legal advice from your lawyer. That's fantastic. Should you then ask for his ethical advice? "Okay, I have a case at law and I have the right to sue but should I exercise that right? Is it an ethical thing to do?" In the crusty old days when lawyers saw themselves as 'professionals' more than they do today, there was a tendency to sidestep this question – or at least to appear to. Strictly speaking, it was a matter for the client. The lawyer told you your rights and you made your own decisions after that. Nowadays, however, with legal practice treated as a 'business' as much as a 'profession,' lawyers openly engage in public debate about the rights and wrongs of suing corporations, insurance companies, doctors and so on. It's highly likely your lawyer will be perfectly happy to discuss the ethics of your situation with you. And there's no reason why you shouldn't listen to his advice. Indeed, you'd be silly not to! But it would equally be a mistake to listen to it *exclusively*, to make your lawyer your sole source of ethical advice. You really need to consult more widely. Only then will you encounter all the different 'takes' on litigation that are circulating in your community. Seek advice on the rights and wrongs of your situation from your trusted friends, mentors and family. They are just as qualified to give advice in this area as your lawyer is! They will help you sort through all the arguments about litigation that are thrown up in the media these days and to work out which arguments have validity and which don't.

But the starting point is, when you are contemplating litigation, you need to ascertain two things:

1. Your legal rights; and
2. Your ethical position.

Your lawyer will be critical to Point 1 and important to Point 2. But Point 2 will also require wider consultation so that, in the end, you are satisfied in yourself that you are doing the right thing.

3 THE REAL ISSUE

Life has taught me that humans are weird creatures. The things we think! The things we say! The things we do! They can be so mysteriously irrational, 'out of character' or plain stubborn! Sometimes a trivial side issue is all it takes to launch two hyped-up humans into a raging dispute that drags on for years. At some point in our lives, we've all had the experience of getting into an argument with someone and not really knowing why. A little way down the track, we suddenly stop and say to ourselves: "Why am I arguing about this? It's just not important enough to be taking up my time!"

When I was a young lawyer, an old lawyer gave me a very precious gift. It wasn't gold or shares or a winning lottery ticket. It was a little piece of advice that he had formulated after decades of dealing with litigating clients. The **Golden Rule** is this:

"Never get into a fight you don't need to be in. And if you need to be in a fight, make sure you win it!"

Like all good advice, it is simple and clear in expression but focuses upon something that can be mighty hard to achieve in practice. When you are locked in battle with an adversary, the testosterone is pumping and it's very hard to take a step back from your dispute and dispassionately ask simple but difficult questions like:

1. What am I fighting about here?
2. Do I really need to be fighting about it?
3. Is there an alternative scenario? Maybe even a "win/win"?

Let me now suggest an hypothesis that would be difficult to prove but may still be true nonetheless: *there are many disputes that are litigated in court that are more about 'clashes of ego' than they are about 'clashes of interests'* (when those interests are dispassionately assessed). At some stage in their dispute, the litigants became locked in combat so heavily that they could see no other solution than slogging it out till the end. They were like a couple of rutting caribou bucks that had gone through all the blustering and the foot-stamping but once the antlers were locked together, there was no practical way of unlocking them apart from a battle to the finish.

THIS IS HARD ADVICE BUT TRUE! All potential litigants should step back from their dispute and ask themselves: What is this fight about? Do I really need to be in it? They need to look at these questions dispassionately. If they can't be dispassionate, they need to acknowledge that fact and get somebody else to assist them in this task. The earlier in the dispute they do this, the better. It will assist either an early resolution of the dispute or a more focussed prosecution of it. If the assessment indicates that there is more ego than substance in the dispute, the question arises: do you want to sacrifice thousands of dollars and a few years of your life to something that's essentially a High School dummy-spit? Of course not! But what if you're being adult about things while your opponent is behaving like an emotional basket case? Well, more on that later in the book ... but it looks like you're in a battle you need to fight and win!

When I was at school, one of my friends used to get into lots of fights. Kids would run up to me and tell me my friend was in a fight at the other end of the playground. Because I was his friend, it was sort of expected that I would go and help him out. I tended not to do this although I did kick one guy he was rolling around on the grass with. The guy's brother then attacked me. Anyway, the odd thing was that, the day after the fight, my friend would be chums with the guy he had been fighting! Huh? I never got that. What was the fight all about? Why couldn't they just skip the fight and go straight to the friendship stage?

This happens in the adult world too. SOME battling litigants are actually more suited to being allies - but they just can't see it. Imagine a filmmaker who has fallen out with another person in the world of entertainment. He has done some work and the invoice is still unpaid. A stalemate exists and he decides he has no other option but to sue. The claim is being defended. These guys are in the same industry. One has a production studio. The other needs to use production facilities. When the lawyers and clients all sit down together and get past the usual chest-thumping, the idea may arise that the dispute could be settled by the studio owner giving some free time in his studio for the filmmaker to work on his current project. It's a good, adult solution that lays the groundwork for an ongoing relationship. And it avoids the matter going to court.

It is often hard for litigants to step back from their dispute and search for win/win solutions. Can you trust your lawyer to do this for you – to help settle your dispute early and thus miss out on lots of juicy fees? Do you *want* your lawyer to do this for you? Some clients interpret a suggestion from their lawyer that an appropriate settlement of their claim might be available without actually going to court as a sign that their lawyer is "doubting them" or "not backing them one hundred per cent." They usually take their business elsewhere. The kind of clients who believe a lawyer should be some kind of intimidating puppet whose strings and vocals they control are bound to be disappointed. Lawyers' professional responsibilities are not restricted to their clients. They also have responsibilities to the court, to their opposing lawyers and to the community in general. It is not a case of "I pay and you do as I say." Nor should it be. It would be a rotten system indeed that allowed lawyers to knowingly lie in court when they were under their client's instructions to do so. That is not our legal tradition and nor do we want it.

In most cases, lawyers are happy to see their clients' disputes resolved on a win/win basis prior to the expense of litigation. That is my experience. It is also my experience, however, that lawyers are very busy people with their minds largely occupied by the time limits and multiple other technical regulations that govern the court process. The awful truth is that your lawyer may not have much time to dispassionately reflect upon your dispute and look for win/win solutions. As a result, you should not rely exclusively on your lawyer to perform this 'thinking' function for you. Try to do it yourself and seek other trusted and wise assistance (although always keep your lawyer fully advised of your plans *before* you execute them so that you avoid doing something that may legally damage your case).

REMEMBER: it's all part of the **Golden Rule**:

"Never get into a fight you don't need to be in. And if you need to be in a fight, make sure you win it!"

4 LITIGATION IS NOT ABOUT WHAT HAPPENED

This is an obvious point but it needs to be understood early. YOU know the history of your legal dispute. YOU know what happened. But, strictly speaking, when your dispute gets into court, it won't be about what happened. It will be about what witnesses are prepared to TESTIFY happened. The version of events given in evidence by sworn witnesses might be the same as your version of events or it might be different. If it's different, the judge will be forced to decide which version the court will accept as the correct one. He or she may not accept your version. OUCH!

How can different people give different evidence about the same events?

Good question. Let's look at it logically.

1. Some of them could be deliberately lying; or
2. They're not deliberately lying but, as a matter of biology, different human brains remember things differently with different focus points and different emphasis.

People who spend a lot of time in court will tell you – sometimes in a whisper – that it's easy to get the impression that deliberate lying by witnesses is a regular occurrence. Maybe not the norm but it does happen. This impression is impossible to prove or disprove. It's conjecture. Make up your own mind whether it's realistic conjecture or not. Certainly, there are a number of successful prosecutions each year for the criminal offence of perjury (lying under oath). Lawyers, of course, are ethically bound NOT to allow the presentation of deliberately false evidence by their clients and witnesses. That would be a fraud upon the court. But if the lawyers are instructed with their client's version of events and there is no objective measure to prove it false, they are right to act on their client's instructions even though their intuition senses that something is amiss. The client is entitled to have his grievance aired in court and to have the court adjudicate according to the law of the land. Who is to say that the lawyer's intuition is correct? Nearly every evening, our television networks broadcast crime dramas where some honest person looks as guilty as sin right up until the last moment when a new and true perspective emerges for the first time, exonerating him completely. The same sort of thing can happen in real life, too!

Much more significant than anxiety about deliberate liars is the wealth of psychological evidence we now have that the human memory is fallible, subject to suggestion and prone to change over time. It is actually a common, if not daily, occurrence in courts around the world to hear witnesses give differing versions of the same events. Most of these people are not lying. They just have different recollections.

So what's the message from all this?

To be honest, the message is no more than a reminder about the reality of life in general and litigation in particular. Your lawyer is quite likely to believe your version of events. That's fine, of course, but what is more important – critical, in fact – is that the judge prefers your version to your opponent's. Central to this will be "the evidence" and, as your legal expert, your lawyer will keep you advised on this as it develops (noting that some evidence may not come to light until after a lawsuit has been filed). Your lawyer will be looking for other evidence that backs up your version of events. It is particularly good if that back-up evidence is objective and independent and recorded in some way at the time of relevant events. What your lawyer WON'T be doing is talking to witnesses and 'coaching' them to change their evidence to match yours!

An ethical dilemma arises if your lawyer informs you that the preponderance of evidence is against your version of what happened. What do you do? Abandon your litigation and let injustice prevail? Or stand up and tell the truth even though you are at serious risk of being disbelieved? We will look at what various philosophers have had to say about this later on in the book.

5 THE LITIGIOUS SOCIETY

So you have a legal problem. You've answered the two questions. Your lawyer says you have a valid case at law (with some ifs, buts and maybes). You are satisfied in yourself that pursuing your legal rights is an ethical course of action. You've taken the time to explore your dispute dispassionately and you've concluded it's a fight you need to be in and one you need to win. So you set to work filing and serving the court documents that launch your litigation. News of your decision therefore becomes public. People talk.

If you have the idea that you will be able to discuss litigation coolly, rationally and sensibly in your community network, FORGET IT! I have tried to do this for decades and never succeeded. Somehow I don't think your chances of success are any better than mine. The sad fact of the matter is that litigation nowadays is a highly political and emotive subject that has become riddled with all manner of fallacious reasoning, sophistry, obfuscation and propaganda to such an extent that it is IMPOSSIBLE to discuss it without voices being raised, tempers flaring and doors being slammed shut. Was it always like this? Well … sort of. The ancient Romans got hot under the collar about litigation at times. But just as togas don't really have collars, they didn't have things like limited liability private corporations, insurance companies and class actions to muddy the waters even more.

Without really knowing what I was getting into, I set myself the task of finding out why it is impossible for modern humans like you and me to have a sensible discussion about the rights and wrongs of litigation. Why does it always end in tears? What I discovered surprised and annoyed me. It will probably have the same effect on you too.

According to my dictionary, a 'paradox' is a statement or proposition that seems self-contradictory or absurd but in reality expresses a possible truth. Whilst studying the place of litigation in modern society, I discovered a neat paradox that strikes at the very heart of our muddle over suing. Here it is:

If every citizen of Utopia were litigious, Utopia would necessarily be a litigious society. But Utopia could still be a litigious society even if not one of its citizens was litigious.

Do you get it? Don't be hard on yourself if the answer is "no." It took me many hours of study and reflection to wake up to the existence of this paradox and what it means. It actually explains why people today can't have a discussion about the rights and wrongs of litigation without coming to blows, either verbal or physical. It shows us why our reasoning on this subject is so muddled. The apparent absurdity of the paradox lies in the second sentence: *how on earth could you have a litigious society if nobody is litigious?* That's crazy! Isn't it?

Actually, it's not. The reason why we can't discuss litigation sensibly today is because we have fallen into the error of using one word - "litigiousness" - to describe two quite different things. Conflict resolution and litigation in particular can be examined on two interrelated levels. The first is the micro level of personal disputation and individual ethics. The second is the macro level of public issues and socio-economic forces. Much of the heat and frustration in the public debate over 'our litigious society' can be attributed to a failure to recognize the existence of these two levels and the confusion that results when logic applicable to one level is inappropriately utilized 'across the board'. For example, many commentators are happy to assume that levels of court litigation that are unacceptably high from a macro point of view ("a litigation explosion") must be caused by individual litigiousness, a micro concept. According to this assumption, because the macro problem is caused by micro factors, you can fix the problem on the micro level. Changes at the micro level will have consequences that will flow up to the macro level – and the problem is solved. However, if this assumption is not correct and the predicted flow from the micro level to the macro level doesn't happen, guess what? You've wasted your time. In my country, Australia, well-paid private consultants have recommended that the government spend public monies attacking micro level litigiousness in order to fix a perceived macro problem at the court registries.[i] Is this throwing much needed public monies down the drain? According to the paradox, it might be. The paradox shows us that the word 'litigiousness' is used to refer to both a personal vice and an operative structural phenomenon that periodically occurs in a society's legal system. The one word refers to both an individual flesh-and-blood person and a huge impersonal social structure set up to resolve a society's disputes. Yes, there can be a causal relationship between these two concepts. That's clear. BUT THERE DOESN'T HAVE TO BE. And that's the critical point. You CAN HAVE a society that is litigious even though none of its citizens are litigious. Let's now look at these issues separately. It's the only way to avoid a teeth-grinding, hair-pulling argument that goes nowhere.

6 THE LITIGIOUS PERSON

In common parlance, a 'litigious' person is someone who will sue 'at the drop of a hat.' Dictionaries tend to define a 'litigious' person as:

- Someone who litigates too much; or
- Someone who is argumentative.

The second usage - that treats 'litigious' as a synonym for 'argumentative' – is old, has become rare in modern discourse and has been dropped by some dictionaries such as Australia's *Macquarie Dictionary*. The meaning I will adopt here is that a litigious person is not just argumentative … a litigious person litigates.

If I described you as "litigious," would you be happy? Would you feel complimented? Of course not! You'd take it as an insult. The word is a 'put down' shrouded with negative connotations. Litigiousness is a vice of excess and litigious people are best avoided. If you are accused of being litigious, one of the nasty little innuendos attached to the label is that you are irrational, maybe even mentally unbalanced. This is quite an old stigma. For example, Mountstuart Elphinstone [1779-1859], the Scottish historian of British India, wrote with disapproval of the "very litigious" Hindu race: "they will persevere in a law-suit till they are ruined."[ii] In 1969, Marvin Katz reported acting as lawyer for a Chinese civil engineer who was injured and instituted personal injuries proceedings. Apparently for cultural reasons, the engineer wanted his 'day in court' and thus refused settlement negotiations. Upon learning of this, the Philadelphia judge ordered a psychiatric examination.[iii] 'Litigious' people are thus often perceived as lacking rationality, as hot-headed, stubborn and unduly sensitive. Their sanity may be called into question, sometimes with severe consequences for their personal liberty and their right of access to the legal system.

Of course, irrationality is itself a subjective concept and, more to the point, does not equal insanity. In any event, the behavior of someone labeled as 'litigious' may be entirely rational, understandable and commendable. It may display the admirable quality of perseverance in the prosecution of a good and just (although unfashionable) cause. On the less admirable side, being notoriously litigious may be an effective strategy if the resultant intimidation produces benefit for the litigant. This is illustrated by the Australian case of the Hoddle Street murderer, Julian Knight. Prison officers alleged he received favorable treatment in prison by continually threatening to sue prison management. The alleged intimidation was such that the State Corrections Minister reportedly investigated whether he could be declared a 'vexatious litigant' (and thereby debarred from suing).[iv] Another example may be corporations or politicians who seek to minimize public scrutiny and criticism through the intimidation that comes from a reputation for being 'quick to sue.' It can be a RATIONAL strategy, all ethical considerations aside.

Mentally ill persons and "vexatious or frivolous litigants"

Of course, there are litigious people who DO suffer from a mental illness that is the cause of their behavior. In psychiatry, as in all fields of human study, terms and classifications vary in time and place. Over the years, the range of medical diagnoses of people who persistently complain has included 'paranoid personality disorder', 'querulous paranoia', 'querulous paranoid state', 'litigious paranoia', 'querulent paranoia', 'paranoia' itself and 'schizophrenia.' This indicates a variety of psychopathology at work. Elements of public display and fanatical righteousness appear essential to paranoid litigants and this is one of the attractions of the legal system for them. They want the whole world to know that they have been wronged. They sometimes become "bush lawyers" as we say in Australia i.e. they gain an extensive knowledge of the law as lay people and steadfastly cling to their legal interpretations. Because of their bizarre public behavior and outlandish claims, they also attract the attention of the media. Unfortunately, the amount of media coverage they are given is out of all proportion to their effect on the overall operation of the legal system and a public misconception can arise that the system is in crisis or under threat.

One recorded example is a fifty-year-old man and his thirty-year-old daughter who believed the United

Kingdom was in the grip of a Masonic conspiracy and so used multiple lawsuits to counter this.[v] It seems that this pair suffered from a mental illness. In any event, they faced an obstacle in the legal system that is designed to deal with litigious people (or, at least, one kind of litigious person). On the same day, both father and daughter were declared "vexatious litigants" and thereby debarred from instituting any more lawsuits without first getting the court's approval. This "vexatious litigant" law is often set out in statutes or in the Rules of Court. Let's not make the mistake of assuming that people declared to be "vexatious litigants" are insane. Some are, some aren't.

When determining whether a lawsuit is "frivolous or vexatious," the court looks at whether it is groundless or faulty or without any prospects of succeeding. In some jurisdictions, the court can also look at the motives of the litigator, his or her litigation history, the wastage of public resources and the harassment of people who are sued for no good cause.

So, in a book like this one addressing the general ethics of litigation, what needs to be said about mentally ill people who repeatedly resort to litigation? I will answer this in a list:

1. I've done the math and these people are a tiny minority of litigants.
2. There is a mechanism in place to deal with them (and other repeat litigants). That mechanism is "vexatious litigant" law. A person who is declared a "vexatious litigant" cannot start litigation without first getting permission from the court.
3. I don't know of any legal jurisdiction anywhere in

the world where vexatious litigants have caused the court system to crumble – or even crack.

4. Noting all of these points, if you are unlucky enough to be the target of a vexatious litigant (particularly one who hasn't yet been officially declared a "vexatious litigant"), your life will be turned upside down for a while and you have my sincere sympathy!

So, when discussing the ethics of litigation, the behavior of mentally ill people and vexatious litigants is a side issue. IT'S NOT THE MAIN GAME. I won't be mentioning it again. From here on, we go back to the world of normal, sane people like you and me who have legal problems that may require litigation. If these sane people are excessively prone to litigate, they may accurately be described as displaying the vice of 'litigiousness.' The question of whether or not YOU are litigious depends on whether or not your litigating is EXCESSIVE. How on earth do you assess that? What does it mean? That you have too many lawsuits to your name? That you are claiming too high a price for damages in your lawsuit? Read on.

7 LAW AND SOCIETY

Actually, let's not read on. Before we have a peek at ancient and modern wisdom about the rights and wrongs of suing, we need to learn a little bit more about litigation itself, what it's for, how it's used and by whom. Litigation can be defined as a structured means of dispute resolution according to law and a way to enforce legal remedies. As such, it is an ESSENTIAL element in every legal system. In an adversarial legal system like in the USA, the UK, Canada and Australia, litigation provides a means for uncovering the facts of a dispute and applying the law of the land to those facts, hopefully ending in a just outcome. There are many different types of litigation with different requirements and arising in very different contexts. It is not easy to equate the filing of a multi-million dollar product liability class action with the filing of a small creditor's petition, for example. There are also many different types of plaintiffs and defendants - from 'natural persons' like you and me to private corporations, statutory bodies, legally recognised churches, charities and not-for-profit organisations. For this reason, making generalizations about litigation and litigants and interpreting litigation statistics must be approached with extreme caution.

Trying to make sense of these things, a group of legal academics in the US began a field of study that came to be known as "Law and Society." One of the pioneers was Marc Gallanter. In 1974, he published an influential article entitled "Why the 'Haves' Come Out Ahead: Speculations on the Limits of Legal Change."[vi] In it, he examined the "basic architecture of the legal system" and how that structure could influence the decisions made by litigants and the outcomes they obtained from their litigation. He separated litigants into "one shotters" and "repeat players." One shotters are infrequent users of the legal system and repeat players are frequent users. One shotters are typically individuals and repeat players are typically corporations. Because of their different attributes and resources, Galanter expected one shotters and repeat players to "play the litigation game" differently. Repeat players have the resources to pursue long-term goals i.e. goals beyond the immediate court case. One shotters, on the other hand, have high stakes in their once-only litigation. The picture that emerges from this analysis is one of power *status quo*, of individuals tending towards the safe, early settlement and corporations manipulating law to their best advantage via "test cases." Reviewing the situation in 1999, Galanter noted the increasing presence of governments, associations and corporations in the court system and their relative immunity from the moral criticism cast upon natural person litigants.[vii]

Another "Law and Society" researcher, Engel, studied this in a small American rural community and noted that the great majority of critics of litigation were actually critics of one *type* of litigation - that involving the law of torts.[viii] Torts is the law of civil wrongs and includes claims for negligence and personal injury. Although the adjective 'litigious' is commonly and inaccurately applied to all torts plaintiffs, the basis of the criticism against them is more that they are greedy, dishonest and opportunistic. They seek to turn life's little accidents into financial windfalls. Engel found such sentiments to be strongly held in the small, rural county he studied. Personal injuries litigation in the county was quite rare - almost ten times less than contract litigation. Strangely, people who sued in contract (e.g. for the repayment of a debt) were not criticized for doing so. The community in general disapproved of one shotter torts plaintiffs but did not extend this disapproval to one shotter contract plaintiffs.

Galanter's one shotter/repeat player analysis has been widely adopted. The Australian Law Reform Commission utilized it when analysing litigants in federal jurisdiction.[ix] It considered one of the advantages of "repeat litigants" is their ability to use strategically all the dispute-resolution mechanisms available, both litigation and its alternatives such as mediation. Because of such strategizing on hidden agendas, it is often difficult to determine who is a "winner" and who a "loser." When a resolution is achieved without recourse to litigation, could that result only have been achieved by threatening litigation? Galanter's characterization of litigation as a "game" is therefore quite apt. My own anecdotal experience suggests that many plaintiff personal injury lawyers perceive insurers as playing out a game in which, for example, they never "get serious" about settlement until litigation is commenced and even then, they never put their best offer first. Undoubtedly, this perception is conveyed to clients and forms part of the basis for any decision to litigate.

Galanter's "law and society" perspective treats litigants as rational actors in a structural system. They are either familiar with that system and its rules or they are not and this affects their behaviour within the system. One shotters are not litigious people. They have a grievance and enter the system because that is what they understand they 'have to do' in order to obtain a realistic resolution. They do not understand the system and many have unrealistic expectations of it. They are guided by advice from repeat players in the form of lawyers. The money-based outcome these litigants obtain frequently leaves them feeling emotionally unsatisfied. Repeat players, on the other hand, see litigation as 'part of the landscape.' They are familiar with it, how it can work against them and how it can work for them. Repeat players are typically people acting in unison as a corporation or organization, but this does not make them immune to moral scrutiny. Because of their repeat use of litigation, repeat players stand to be labelled "litigious" when the level of litigating becomes "excessive." This, of course, is debatable in any given case. A repeat player who litigates from time to time on the basis of legally sound arguments may not be viewed as litigious. I suggest, however, that a repeat player who litigates strategically on what it understands to be legally weak cases is indeed likely to be litigious. That repeat player may be seeking to delay its payment, to oppress its opponent, to outlive a geriatric or sick opponent, to gain publicity or political mileage or any other similar advantage.

In summary, the "law and society" perspective does not view personal litigiousness as necessarily a major factor in the operation of the legal system. It does not refute the possibility of social litigiousness, but sees it arise as a rational response by one shotters and a means by powerful repeat players to maintain their power. Galanter also contends that the 20th century saw a collision between two "master trends," namely an expansion of available legal remedies and a rise to dominance by organizational entities.[x]   Even way back in 1992, according to the Bureau of Justice Statistics, a survey of the 75 largest counties in the USA revealed that 67.5 per cent of plaintiffs in contract cases were business organisations such as insurance companies, banks, finance companies and businesses.[xi] In torts cases, only 6 per cent of plaintiffs were business organizations. The hype we read in the media about tort law and a "crazy" legal system needs to be examined carefully. Who is making the criticism? Why? Can they prove the things they claim? Do they even try or do they just pick accusations out of the air? Could it be that the criticism is merely a self-serving attempt by an organization or special interest group to prune the growth of remedies favouring individual citizens?

8 INHERITED WISDOM ON THE 'RIGHTS' AND 'WRONGS' OF SUING

Litigation is way older than Facebook. It goes back thousands of years in many different cultures around the world. Happily for us, that means that we can tap into thousands of years of diverse human experience and wisdom on this very subject. Most people don't bother – and that's understandable. When you are embroiled in litigation that could "make or break" you, your focus is necessarily on the task at hand. You don't have time to look up what some ancient Greek philosopher said about suing. And what would he know anyway? He lived in a sheep-herding economy that made war with swords and spears. Life has become a whole lot more complicated. That's true, of course. But ancient peoples were just as human as we are and some things never change, especially at the basic level of what is right and what is wrong. An arrow and a nuclear missile may seem totally different but they are both deliberate means of killing enemies. The fundamental motivation behind them is exactly the same. Anyway, let's now take a brief look at some litigation wisdom, both old and new, and you can make up your own mind. A mountain of words has been written on the subject of ethics – check your State or County library and you'll see what I mean – so my summaries here are meant to be as short and succinct as possible.

Plato

Plato was born in Athens in around 428 BC. To him, ethics was something derived from the intellect and study. Suing, in his view, was a sign of bad education. In *The Republic*, he criticized the man who relied on others to give him justice without any idea how far "higher and nobler" it is "so to order his life as to be able to do without a napping judge."[xii] Plato was not an admirer of Athenian democracy and took a dim view of its court system. This is not surprising as the courts were partly politicized and corrupted by "sycophancy," the practice of powerful private persons intervening in other's litigation, supposedly in the public interest but often to gain a personal profit or advantage for themselves. In Athens, your lawsuit was likely to fail unless you obtained the support of an influential citizen who would sit in court with you and, by his presence, intimidate the judge and your opponent. Your opponent, of course, would strive to have his own power broker to balance things up. With equal intimidation from each side, the judge was then free to be impartial and make a balanced judgment. That was the theory for some, anyway. To Plato, however, using the court system meant surrendering some or all of your independence and this was to be avoided. Living life in such a way as to avoid the need for litigation is no doubt good advice. It may even be achievable in small, close-knit, homogenous communities where everybody knows everybody else, where values are shared and where non-violent, 'shaming' pressure can be brought to bear on wrongdoers outside the legal system. Whether it is achievable in today's mass, anonymous and heterogeneous society is another thing altogether. The population of classical Athens was about 200,000 whereas New York City today is heading for 8 and a half million. But Plato surely deserves a tick for one piece of good advice: stay out of court if you can!

Aristotle and "Virtue Ethics"

Aristotle was born in 384 BC and was a student of Plato. Their views on ethics, however, were quite different. Aristotle saw a difference between 'doing the right thing' and 'moral virtue.' That difference was found not in the act itself but in the disposition of the doer. If you perform right action in the way that people of just character do, this qualifies as moral virtue. On the other hand, if you do the right thing begrudgingly or in a self-serving way, this would not constitute moral virtue. The way you do things was important to Aristotle because he believed that virtues could be acquired by training: "by doing just acts we become just." His virtue-based ethics did not debar recourse to litigation and sometimes required it, always done in a manner befitting "just and temperate" people. Seeing moral virtue as a mean between two vices, Aristotle considered that each person should strive to act "at the right times, and on the right occasions, and towards the right persons, and with the right object, and in the right fashion."[xiii] Thus, depending upon the individual circumstances, litigation may or may not be virtuous action. Aristotle described one variety of "just action" as that which provides rectification of imbalances between loss and gain. Thus, he argued, disputants go to court because the judge is meant to be "a living embodiment of that which is just" and can restore a proper balance between the litigants. Obviously, this theory requires a judicial system untainted by bias and corruption.

Confucius (551-479 BC)

Confucius say wise man never litigates. That was a joke, actually. Confucius said no such thing. Indeed, at times during his career, maybe when he was the governor of a town or the Minister of Crime in China, he was required to hear and settle disputes, somewhat like a judge. "In hearing litigations, I am like any other body," he said. "What is necessary, however, is to cause the people to have no litigations."[xiv] Confucius believed that litigation would not be necessary if everybody behaved properly. This book is not the place to explore the intricate worldview of this famous Oriental philosopher. But the *Confucian Analects* contain much wisdom for potential litigators. For example, somebody once put to Confucius the proposition that one should recompense injury with kindness, a kind of 'turning the other cheek.' Confucius wasn't impressed. He responded with a question: if you did that, what would you recompense kindness with? He preferred the following advice: "recompense injury with justice, and recompense kindness with kindness."[xv]

Clearly, Confucius thought it appropriate to respond to attacks of ill will by going to court and seeking the justice of the law. There are, of course, cases where it is perfectly clear that one party has acted maliciously or aggressively against another party whose behavior has been entirely benign. Confucius' advice covers that scenario well. But there are many cases where both parties to a dispute feel aggrieved by the behavior of the other party with some level of justification. These battling parties go to court, each fervently seeking justice. But exactly what *is* justice? In my experience, many litigants have a very simple definition: *if I win and get what I want, that's justice! If I lose, that's injustice!* This definition will be accurate in a certain percentage of cases. For the rest, all it does is display a lack of capacity for introspection, a lack of the ability to imagine oneself in somebody else's boots. Here again, Confucius has some wise advice: "the superior man in everything considers righteousness to be essential."[xvi] In other words, you should always be fair, especially when you are in a position of power. Of course, some people use sophistry (clever arguments) to convince themselves and others that what they want is really nothing more than justice when, in fact, this is not the case if examined objectively. Confucius disapproved of this. "Specious words confound virtue," said he.[xvii] Inventing excuses for our behavior is to be avoided.

The Buddha (b. 563 BC)

"One thing only do I teach, suffering and its end to reach." As a religion, Buddhism has a strong focus on the individual and his or her personal journey of liberation from the unsatisfactoriness of a life where everything is fleeting and impermanent. The Buddha taught using two levels of truth. The first is the conventional level of truth that refers to persons and groups of persons and their actions over time. The second is the ultimate level where phenomena are seen in their atomic, constituent forms, rising and passing away in quick succession in accordance with prevailing conditions. In a sense, it's like physics where conventional eyes see a 'dining table' but ultimate eyes see an ever-changing mass of atoms. Litigation clearly belongs in the world of conventional truth. Given that the Buddha established a large following of monks and nuns known as the *Sangha*, it was inevitable that disputes would arise and be brought before him for adjudication. That is exactly what happened. During his lifetime, he oversaw the development of a large set of rules governing the conduct of monks and nuns. Processes were established whereby aggrieved parties could bring a complaint against monks and nuns and have the matter openly aired and settled by adjudication. In other words, the Buddha was not opposed to litigation at all and treated it as a useful tool for maintaining order and harmony amongst his followers. In the Bhaddāli Sutta, a monk named Bhaddāli asked the Buddha about litigation.[xviii] The Buddha's answer implies that it was important for the *Sangha* to correct the behavior and attitude of errant monks and litigation was a way of doing this. If the errant monk did not see the error of his ways and 'stuck to his guns,' the Buddha said that the litigation should not be settled too quickly. On the other hand, if the errant monk did acknowledge his wrongdoing and agree to act rightly in the future, the litigation could be settled quickly. Ultimately, of course, if a monk or nun refused to follow the rules of the *Sangha*, he or she would be expelled.

Ancient Rome

In ancient Rome, the occurrence of periodic 'litigation explosions' is recorded along with public and government concern about the stirring up of disputation. Overall, however, litigation was not considered intrinsically bad. It was seen as ethically acceptable to sue for a just cause, provided that the individual did not do so excessively.

This is very similar to the situation we face today. It's worth noting, though, that a good education in the Classical World contained heavy doses of the study of Rhetoric or the art of persuasion. But the true rhetorician was *vir bonus dicendi peritus* [a morally good man skilled in speaking] and not just a self-serving windbag. Part of being a Roman citizen (if you were lucky enough to actually be one) was the expectation that you could stand up and verbally defend your actions in public if required to do so. The modern philosopher, Peter Singer, says the same thing i.e. that part of an ethical life is the willingness and ability to justify your actions to others.[xix] This is an area in which many modern one shotters fall down: they can't publicly articulate the moral justification for their litigation and 'leave the talking' to their lawyer who is often little better, he or she only wanting to talk about 'legal rights' for fear of going beyond their area of expertise. So the moral dimension is left undiscussed giving all and sundry the false impression that there *is* no moral justification for the litigation.

Christianity and the Sermon on the Mount

When Christianity began to take hold in the Roman Empire, the early Christians had a real problem on their hands: should they sue to enforce their rights in the Roman court system knowing that they would have to take pagan oaths to do so or should they strictly follow Christ's counsel to 'turn the other cheek,' to forgive one's enemies and to forgive debts. In the Sermon on the Mount, Christ had preached: "And if any man will sue thee at the law, and take away thy coat, let him have thy cloak also."[xx]

From the reign of the emperor Justinian - himself a Christian - a view took hold that litigation was intrinsically bad and to be avoided - even if the claim itself was good. This view became an undercurrent that never completely managed to stop Christians from suing, obviously because many were unable to accept 'putting up with it' as the only response to injustices thrust upon them. In medieval Christendom, however, demand existed for ways to resolve disputes without classical court litigation. Elaborate laws were developed for trials by ordeal and battle and compurgation. These dispute-resolution methodologies involved the taking of Christian oaths and the engagement of *Judicium Dei* [the judgment of God]. They channeled dispute resolution away from the litigating courtroom and back into 'the hands of God.' Compurgation involved oaths as to the defendant's good character being accepted as evidence against a claim. Trial by ordeal could be by fire, hot water or cold water. In ordeal by fire, the subject either held or walked over red-hot metal. Any injury indicated guilt. In ordeal by hot water, the subject plunged his or her arm into boiling water. Again, injury indicated guilt. In ordeal by cold water, the subject was thrown into a lake. If the subject floated, he or she was considered guilty. Trial by battle arose from pre-Christian roots. The pagan Vikings, for example, designated a 'fighting square' – often an island in a river – where people with a dispute could agree to go and fight to the death with no legal consequences arising from the homicide. The lack of legal consequences, however, did not stop the relevant families from bearing grudges that would erupt again later on. If a fit, young man from one family killed an older man from another family in the fighting square, the aggrieved family would wait until the killer was himself old. He would then be challenged by a fit, young man from the deceased's family who would return the punishment meted out to his kinsman. The Christians watered this savage practice down. Their version originally involved disputants each taking an oath and then fighting for a set time with leather shield and cudgel. At the height of the Middle Ages, you were allowed to choose someone else to do the fighting for you. This substitute fighter was the *campio conductivus* or 'champion.' The champion was a professional who had to be paid. He was unpopular for this reason and the term *campio conductivus* was often used as an insult. A modern parallel is the notion that lawyers and advertising agencies are just 'hired guns' who will do anything for anyone as long as they get their money. This negative anti-lawyer view is reminiscent of Plato - not only does litigation involve giving up one's independence to the judiciary, it also usually requires a *de facto* surrender of control to lawyers. On this view, suing is wrong because, by reason of either law or practicality or a combination of both, it involves getting others to fight one's own battles and worse, turns one into a client of high-cost legal specialists whose ethics are not known or understood. As the old Swedish proverb says: 'if you take the Devil into your boat, you have to row him ashore.' In our fast –paced modern life and with our ever-growing array of complex laws and regulations, however, just how one could successfully do without specialist lawyers is no easy question to answer!

Christian scriptural disapproval of litigation and a more general disapproval of its attendant social discord gave rise to laws against barratry, maintenance and champerty. 'Barratry' involved "habitually moving, exciting or maintaining suits or quarrels, whether at law or not."

'Maintenance' involved "assisting a party in litigation without lawful justification" and 'champerty' was doing so for some form of profit. These criminal offences were rarely invoked in modern times and have actually been abolished in many jurisdictions on the grounds that the mischief they address is better controlled by vexatious litigant law, the awarding of legal costs against a party and the regulation of legal professional standards. Furthermore, some assisting of parties in litigation - through legal aid schemes and commercial arrangements - is now considered commendable if it increases access to the justice system for people with meritorious claims.

In summary, you may have some Christian friends who will NEVER sue and some who are perfectly happy to sue. Now you know why. The ones who will never sue are very much in the minority these days.

Immanuel Kant [1724-1804] and the Categorical Imperative

Kant was a German philosopher who believed that reason is the source of morality. He is famous for formulating his "Categorical Imperative" which states: "Act only according to that maxim whereby you can, at the same time, will that it should become a universal law." Kant believed that you should act in accordance with reason, regardless of the possible consequences for you and regardless of your own personal feelings. In the context of the legal system, this means that, when you are right and 'have the law on your side', you MUST enforce your legal rights, if necessary by suing, EVEN IF you don't really want to or can't be bothered or would rather just go on a holiday to Hawaii and forget the whole damn thing. According to Kant, if you are in the right (taking a reasoned and universalistic view of the matters in dispute) then you MUST sue or you will be an agent of wrong and your agency will adversely affect others in the future. Adherents of such Kantian philosophy today may be in danger of diagnosis as 'querulous paranoids' with an overvalued idea of being in possession of the truth and an inescapable desire to correct the wrong. To be fair to Kant, however, his philosophy could in appropriate circumstances lead to the conclusion that one's duty is *not* to enforce a legal right. This may occur where an inclination to sue is present but acting upon it would transform a purely selfish motive into a universal law. For example, it may be materially advantageous and/or personally satisfying for an entrepreneur to sue a Jewish competitor on objectively nebulous grounds in a biased Nazi court. Most would agree, however, that the application of the Categorical Imperative would deem this morally wrong.

Utilitarianism

This view of ethics arose in the seventeenth and eighteenth centuries largely through the writings of Jeremy Bentham and John Stuart Mill. In the modern world, Peter Singer counts himself as a utilitarian. In a nutshell, they argue that actions that produce more benefits than harm are right and those that don't are wrong. This is often described as "the greatest happiness principle" meaning that something is ethically correct to the extent that it produces a greater balance of pleasure over pain for the greatest number of people involved in the issue. Putting this into action in the practical world requires a detailed and balanced examination of whom the action helps and whom it hurts. One of the major criticisms of utilitarianism is that it's impractical for use in everyday life, that nobody has time to stop and reflect deeply on how what they are about to do will help or harm themselves and others. As humans, we just don't work that way! In the context of litigation, however, this criticism loses much of its clout because the instituting of legal proceedings is a slow process that gives ample opportunity for reflection. The would-be litigant generally takes lengthy advice from family, friends, colleagues, lawyers and other professionals and experts. Negotiation is often attempted. The decision to litigate is a serious one and the filing of a plaint in court only occurs after significant preparation. My own anecdotal experience is that litigators do go through a type of utilitarian analysis of their actions. This produces comments like "I don't want the same thing to happen to anybody else." There is a substantial body of research indicating that litigants seek 'moral vindication' and social and emotional benefits from litigation. This is in contrast to their lawyers who have their eyes firmly fixed on the money side of things i.e. the damages and remedies their clients are entitled to claim.

Another criticism of Utilitarianism is that, whilst one act in a particular set of circumstances may meet the test of providing the greatest happiness for the greatest number of people, if everybody took up performing that act in general, disastrous consequences would ensue. Mill himself discussed this in the context of lying. Whilst one particular lie in a specific situation may be generally beneficial, if everyone adopted the rule that lying is acceptable, this would lead to disastrous results. Hence, one needed to examine not only the act in question but the issue of what would happen if the act transformed into a rule. This explains the contrast between "act utilitarianism" and "rule utilitarianism" you will read about in modern ethics textbooks.

Rights and Social Contracts

Our ancient forebears spoke a lot about 'right' and 'wrong' and 'duty' but never about people's 'rights.' The idea of people having things called 'rights' was something that crystallised in Europe in the seventeenth and eighteenth centuries. The printing press had been refined and was in full swing. The illiterate peasants of the Dark Ages, violently subjugated through their responsibilities to pay taxes and provide cannon-fodder for the armies of the aristocracy, were now more educated and more aware that the aristocracy needed them in the same way that a parasite needs a host. Suddenly, the notion of 'responsibilities' wasn't the one-way street it had always looked like. There was a 'social contract' at work. Sure, the 'have-nots' had responsibilities (that caused them to surrender up some of their freedom). But the 'haves' had responsibilities, too - to put it another way, the 'have-nots' had rights that did not rely for their existence upon the whim, virtue or largesse of the 'haves.' These rights – or at least some of them – came from a higher plane of authority and were thus said to be natural and inalienable and to exist even if they weren't actually 'the law of the land.' To ignore them was to break the social contract that existed between the State and the subject, the powerful and the weak and to invite rebellion and revolution. So postulated writers like Thomas Hobbs, John Locke and Jean Jacque Rousseau. The highly venerated law of *habeas corpus*, a remedy against unlawful detention, had been around since the fourteenth century but was first codified in the seventeenth century in this atmosphere. Nowadays, we sometimes hear complaints about "all this talk of rights and no mention of responsibilities." In the particular context being discussed, I often agree with the complaint. But I strongly object to attempts to demonise the weak in society and to harken back to 'the good old days' when the weak knew their place. If their overlord was a virtuous man, they prospered. If he was an ethical zero, they starved. In a world where we surrender so much of our freedom to a State apparatus that is heavily lobbied by powerful and wealthy interest groups, the weak deserve basic consideration. And they should be able to sue if they don't get it.

Communitarian Ethics

A Communitarian is someone who focuses less upon the individual and his or her rights and concerns and more upon the community that has nurtured and supported and given meaning to individual existence. Communitarians feel that too much talk about individual rights and individual sovereignty blinds us to the fact that we are not 'islands' but part of an intricate community web that is actually the foundation of our self-image and largely defines our individual potentialities. The health of that community web is considered more crucial than individual rights and desires. Communitarianism is not so much an answer to ethical problems as an outlook from which to view and critique them.

In the context of litigation, something like the

communitarian perspective has been around for thousands of years. It usually manifests itself in the form of concerns about social discord and a breakdown in social cohesion. The Romans were concerned about excessive bouts of litigation from time to time, as were the later Europeans who passed laws against barratry and champerty. I dare not call the Roman emperors "communitarians" because they were probably more focussed upon maintaining their own sectional power base than upon fostering a fair and equitable community balance. As a philosophy, communitarianism is a relatively modern reaction to the perceived excesses of modern liberal ideologies that are centred squarely upon the individual.

There are many and varied communitarian perspectives. They are quite capable of viewing litigation as a necessary tool in the community's need to give vent to grievances and to maintain checks and balances. They are also most likely to view 'excessive' litigation as a symptom of deeper community issues that may require a more considered response than the knee-jerk reaction of placing limits on the ability to sue.

Stand up for yourself and you stand up for others

There is another approach to litigation ethics that has a communitarian ring to it and may produce a moral requirement to litigate. This is the reasoning that, by standing up for ourselves, we stand up for others. It is at the root of the argument routinely made by plaintiff lawyer groups that litigation serves society by terminating 'ongoing harms' and by deterring 'future harms, known and unknown.' This approach fits very comfortably with litigation against human rights violations, unsafe manufacturing and fraudulent or reckless behavior. It also supports suing on principle in smaller matters where, for example, a wrongdoer is unrepentant and not willing to cease unethical conduct. It is more difficult to employ, however, to justify the minor 'slip and fall in the scout hall' plaint or the insurance company's raising of fully and properly disclosed policy exclusions against a claim.

Insurance Companies versus Plaintiff Lawyer groups

An awful lot of the heat in the litigation debate comes from an ongoing feud between the insurance industry and plaintiff lawyer groups. The insurance industry makes a profit (and sometimes a very GOOD profit) by selling insurance against loss. Obviously, it suits their bottom line if the losses are kept to a minimum. This is why they are forever assessing their "risk" and adding in "policy exclusions" on events deemed too likely to happen and too expensive to fix up. On the other hand, plaintiff lawyers are in the business of identifying loss situations where the loser is entitled to sue for compensation and where there are "deep pockets" capable of coughing up that compensation when the court awards it. They sound like natural born enemies but it's probably closer to the truth to argue like those theologians who insist that, if you have a god, you need a devil as well. I'll let you decide who is who! I've actually worked on both sides of this divide and they are all pretty nice people, as a matter of fact! But you won't find an insurance industry representative endorsing the early Christian view that making a claim is an intrinsic moral wrong. Indeed, where would the insurance industry be without the concepts of loss, reimbursement, claim and subrogation?

Periodically, the insurance industry will lobby governments for "tort reform." They want the government to pass laws limiting the amounts people can sue for in torts claims like negligence and personal injury cases. These lobbying sessions are often begun with an assertion that there is a "litigation explosion" that is threatening to make all insurance premiums more expensive. Sometimes the claim is made that the very viability of the insurance industry is under threat. Regrettably, such claims are easy to make but not always easy to prove. It is interesting to examine the ethical arguments the insurance industry raises against policy claimants and litigants. In my experience, they invariably champion Platonic individualism and denounce 'claim and blame.' They lament the "reduction in people's willingness to take personal responsibility for their own situation and to accept misfortune"[xxi] and the "increased expectation that 'if something happens, someone pays.'"[xxii] There is often also mention of forcing premiums up and making insurance more expensive for everybody else.

In reply, plaintiff lawyers will allege hypocrisy, either pointing to high insurance profit reports or, if profits are down, to alleged industry mismanagement. Insurance has been known to be a cyclical business with an "up" cycle and a "down" cycle. Plaintiff lawyers and some economists contend that the insurance industry mismanages its finances during the "up" cycle and is then caught short when the "down" cycle hits. The industry should then take heed of its own advice to "take personal responsibility for their own situation and to accept misfortune" instead of seeking government and community assistance to stabilize their profit margins. Plaintiff lawyers argue that citizens should not lose their rights to compensation just to suit the shareholders of insurance companies.

I'm sure Aristotle would have something interesting to say on "tort reform." When the insurance industry argues that individuals should 'accept misfortune,' Aristotle may in some circumstances agree as a matter of individual ethics. Once it was agreed that the litigation of a particular one shotter is not virtuous, is it then appropriate for the lawmaker to prohibit future litigation of that type by anyone else? Aristotle would view these questions as entirely separate. In his outlook, it makes no difference whether a good man has injured a bad man or *vice versa* - it treats the parties as equal and asks only whether one has done wrong and the other has suffered wrong. The focus of the lawmaker should be the justness of the law and not the decency of the law-user. I would rephrase this as: when amending the law, keep your eyes on the macro factors and not the micro factors otherwise you might legislate an injustice. I concede that an injustice might be justifiable where, for example, it allowed fairer distribution of limited resources. If that were the case, however, the argument should be made ON THOSE GROUNDS rather than by attacking the characters of one shotters, something that will vary with each case.

Corporations and other artificial legal entities

As we saw earlier, a great deal of litigation is NOT commenced by natural persons like you and me but by artificial legal entities such as corporations. This is particularly so in areas like contract law, bankruptcy law and intellectual/property rights. Plato wouldn't have known a limited liability corporation even if he tripped over one. They didn't actually exist in the realm of private commerce until King Magnus Eriksson of Sweden gave a Royal Charter to *Stora Kopparberg* in 1347 and, in the centuries to come, the granting of Royal Charters to the Dutch East India Company and British East India Company. And let's be a little blunt here: companies were invented as things that flesh-and-blood people could hide behind. It was a way to limit their liability and increase profits. In time, ambitious entrepreneurs would start up a company to pursue an economic goal. If things went well, they paid lower taxes. If things went disastrously, the company would be "liquidated" but their own personal assets would be safe. That was one of the main reasons why the concept of a company arose and why companies became so prolific and successful. What would life be like today if there had been no British East India Company or Ford Motor Company? Nowadays, of course, the picture has become a little more complicated. In some places, governments have legislated to prune back the "limited liability" of shareholders and directors.

Corporations are artificial rather than natural persons. Is it possible to question the ethics of an artificial person? Yes, of course it is! They're not robots but natural persons acting in unison under a company name. Their ethics can be judged in the same way that yours and mine can be. Many company boards seek to deflect criticism of their ethics by pointing out that they are legally required to maximize the financial return to their shareholders - as if that can somehow excuse using child labor in the Third World or dumping toxic waste into river systems. It is a feeble excuse that has spawned moves to amend corporation law to water down the emphasis upon shareholder returns.[xxiii]

So, a fair analysis of litigation can't just focus on people who have an accident and sue for damages under the law of torts. It's vital to look at corporations too. I'm not even going to touch the issue of litigation by and on behalf of Big Tobacco. Two other examples will suffice to show that companies sometimes litigate in ethical shadowlands. The first is where corporations appear to seek out the 'deep pockets' of insurance companies (a frequent allegation made against natural person one shotters). In the corporate world, this can involve Directors & Officers liability insurance, a policy that is taken out by corporations to protect themselves against legal action brought against them for alleged wrongful acts of their own employees. Of course, a bank taking out a D & O insurance policy would argue that it is merely taking precautions against potential loss. When lodging a claim under the policy, it would argue that it is merely enforcing the contract between itself and the insurance company. What could be wrong with that? However, just as flesh-and-blood torts plaintiffs are often suspected of greed, the bank will face suspicion that it may have scapegoated some of its employees to recover a loss the actual cause of which was systemic failure rather than employee vice or misconduct. Certainly, insurance companies sometimes have a different interpretation of the events leading to the loss and are not always willing to accept that they are liable under the terms of the policy. In 1983, Lockheed sued its D&O insurer for $8 million after some of its executives admitted to bribing foreign officials. In the action, Lockheed also asked for punitive damages of $10 million from its insurer![xxiv]

The second example is corporate litigation in the field of intellectual property. It has been alleged that certain companies in the United States purchased trademarks and patents and used them for no other purpose than to threaten other existing businesses with litigation. One such company, Refac Technology Development Corporation, initiated two thousand breach-of-patent lawsuits and threatened a thousand more. This development was noted with some concern by the Law Reform Commission of New South Wales when it reviewed that state's old barratry, maintenance and champerty laws.[xxv]

In summary, a balanced examination of the ethics of decisions to litigate must encompass *all* decision-makers, be they natural or artificial persons. The approach is essentially the same for both.

9 COMMENTS ON LITIGATION, SOCIAL HARMONY AND THE RULE OF LAW

"There's so much litigating going on these days, it's terrible!"

Have you heard comments like that when you are out and about in your community? I certainly have. It's a comment I hear at the tennis club but not in the local Chamber of Commerce. In the Chamber of Commerce, entrepreneurs tell me it's too expensive to litigate and everyone avoids it. So, who's right? Is there a lot of litigating going on or isn't there? I won't answer this question now. Instead, I'm going to focus on the original comment. If there is a lot of litigating going on, *so what?* What's wrong with that? Would you prefer that disputing people took the law into their own hands, fought each other in the streets or dueled to death like in the Wild West? Many people don't like to see social disharmony and disputation at all. They think that people should just "get on with one another." Arguing and disputation is to be avoided altogether.

Interestingly, the exact opposite is taught in all the Masters of Business Administration courses that are flourishing in our universities. In those courses, it is invariably taught that social disharmony is an energizing force that underpins innovation and overcomes inertia and apathy. We argue with each other and thereby fully explore all angles rather than just nodding like "yes men." Providing the social disharmony does not reach violent and destructive levels, it is actually considered a positive and healthy sign. So the next time you hear "there's so much litigating going on these days," you might just as validly remark "thank heavens for that" as "it's terrible." Much more information is needed to assess whether the situation is ethically good or bad.

One of the grand oddities of public discourse these days is the fact that the people who denounce and condemn litigation are often the same people who crow about the importance of "the rule of law" in our democratic society. They don't seem to notice the discordance in their views. LITIGATION LIES AT THE VERY HEART OF THE RULE OF LAW THEORY. Without the prospect of litigating about the law, its meaning and how it ought to be applied, the rule of law concept is mere hollow rhetoric. Some of these odd people go on to argue that citizens should have legal rights, by all means, but they shouldn't be educated about them lest they be tempted to enforce them. You can't have it both ways! Either we're an educated society with enforceable laws or we're not.

10 MEDIATION VS 'YOUR DAY IN COURT'

In my lifetime, great strides have been made within the court system in forcing parties to try and settle their dispute by mediation before actually litigating it. If it is successful, this saves time and expense and lessens the workload of the courts. It is a good development from that point of view. However, a tendency has arisen to consider every mediated settlement as a positive statistic – and I don't think that's true. I have seen cases where litigants have effectively been bullied into settling their claim on a basis they actually consider unjust because the mediators have frightened them about:

- the cost risks of litigation (in some countries, a losing litigant pays the legal costs of the winning litigant);
- the uncertainty of evidence ("it's your word against his"); and
- other unknowns like the attitudes of the judges and jurors.

These litigants had been in search of 'right' and 'wrong' – the language of justice. There was very little talk about this, however, and instead, they were presented with 'risk'

– the language of insurance pragmatism. They went home that evening feeling totally empty, their heads ringing with the message that justice was reserved for the rich and the reckless. But their mediated settlement showed up in the success column of the court's annual report. Does it really belong there? Or is it more indicative of a society's failure to provide its citizens with a fast and affordable way to debate openly the rights and wrongs of community behaviour?

11 SHOULD I SUE? HOW TO DECIDE THIS MAJOR QUESTION

The medieval Christian view that litigation is an inherent evil has largely been replaced in our society by the older classical view of litigation, namely, that suing to enforce a valid claim is ethical, provided one doesn't do it excessively. Hence, the word 'litigious' now means more than just 'contentious.' It means 'excessively prone to litigate.' With the increase of education in society has come a growing awareness that citizens have 'rights.' This is consistent with the important Rule of Law principle that requires citizens to know the law and obey it and, if they do not know a specific law, to know how to find out about it. But 'having rights' does not mean 'being right.' I argue that confusion results when people fail to see the distinction between law and ethics. The decision to litigate is one that should be made on both legal and ethical grounds and the reasoning used must be both valid and relevant. If that sounds like walking through a minefield, don't worry! I'm now going to share with you my own "rule of thumb" test for deciding whether or not to sue. It's not a purebred test but a mongrel one, combining several different ethical methodologies. That's its strength, in my opinion. It looks at the issue from different perspectives and can easily be adapted to suit the unique features of each case. And no two cases are exactly alike! So here it is:

Should I sue?

1. **Is my claim legally valid?**
2. **Is my claim morally valid?**
3. **Is my motivation virtuous?**
4. **Who will be affected by my litigation?**
5. **Will the beneficial consequences of my litigation outweigh the adverse consequences for those affected?**

Question 1: Is my claim legally valid?

Your lawyer will be pivotal in helping you answer this question. You'll be paying for this advice so make sure you get a good lawyer (one who is ethical, experienced in your legal problem area and in the art of litigation) and make sure you fully understand the advice you are being given. Don't be afraid to ask questions! You won't look "stupid" if you do so! The fact is: you aren't familiar with the workings of the legal system and a good lawyer will explain from the basics up rather than just babbling at you in legalese.

Question 2: Is my claim morally valid?

Even when you have a good legal case, you still have to ask this question. So I can sue but *should* I? What is the right thing to do with my rights? By all means, ask your lawyer for his opinion on the ethics of your suing. But don't stop there! Ask other trusted sources as well: family, friends, mentors. You and they are just as much an expert on "right and wrong" as any smarty-pants lawyer. The remaining questions in this "rule of thumb" will help focus your thoughts.

Questions 3: Is my motivation virtuous?

This is a tricky one and needs to be handled carefully. To answer this question HELPFULLY requires two things: INTROSPECTION and REALISM. Whilst we may never truly know what is motivating us at a deeper level, an attempted conscious examination of inner motive can help clarify the goal being sought. If we know what we are truly seeking, we may find that litigating is not the best way to attain it. The tricky part is that modern psychology (and some traditions like ancient Buddhism) suggest that an awful lot of our mental activity is based upon basic drives and motivations that can easily be painted as "bad" or "unwholesome." In other words, it is part of the human condition to think un-virtuous thoughts. Like it or not, we're not saints! Part of our reality is thinking tainted with things like desire for revenge and desire for money. Not good, but so what? If I sue someone who has defrauded me horribly and I occasionally ponder how nice it will be to see the cad humiliated and having to pay the money back in court or what I'll do with the money when I get it, do those moments of technically "unwholesome" thought invalidate the correctness of my decision to litigate? I say not. I'm not a saint and my mind is prone to the occurrence of nominally "bad" or impure thoughts from time to time. If I were to throw my hands in the air and abandon the litigation because of "impure thoughts," that would display a total ignorance of the human condition and a lack of realism. Aristotle might say that my motivation shows that I am not a virtuous man but this doesn't make my cause any less just. On the other hand, if I am suing a charitable organization for an accident in their meeting hall that didn't happen and I am lying just to get my hands on some money, I have to face the fact that my motivation is not virtuous, my cause is not just and, according to all the major religious and ethical traditions of the human species, bad consequences will accrue to me as a result of this. Period. There are many grey areas too, of course. Maybe I am really suing for the return of some personal item or just want an official apology. Knowing these things, those particular goals may be better achieved through means other than litigation. To summarise, it's important to examine your inner motivation when litigating but be careful not to overreact: the presence of some ugly thoughts doesn't necessarily mean that justice is not on your side!

Question 4: Who will be affected by my litigation?

This question asks you to identify all the people who will be affected by your litigation. There could be animals affected too, don't forget! Indeed, some litigation is all about animals! These people and living beings are often referred to as the "stakeholders." Stakeholders aren't just anyone or anything: they have to be impacted by your litigation and have a legitimate interest or concern in its outcome. Pure sticky-beaks need not apply! You should compile a list of these stakeholders and what their interest in your litigation is. When talking about court cases, stakeholders often include:

- one's dependents;
- one's opponent;
- the lawyers;
- any witnesses;
- the court; and
- the community as a whole.

Question 5: Will the beneficial consequences of my litigation outweigh the adverse consequences for those affected?

This, of course, is a utilitarian costs/benefits analysis. Cast your mind back to our discussion of the utilitarians and their desire to do the most good for the most number of stakeholders? This is where you examine the good consequences and the bad consequences of your litigation and weigh them up. Overall, will more good be achieved and will more stakeholders be benefited? As Confucius would say, you should undertake this exercise in a spirit of fairness or it will simply amount to a worthless self-justification. But don't hesitate to be robust where appropriate too! Remember that sometimes what is good for someone tastes like bitter medicine and is disliked. This exercise is not about giving people what they want. It's meant to be at a deeper level and beyond the superficial likes and dislikes that we often cling to as part of our social personas. It's meant to be about what is objectively beneficial, what is "right" for individuals and what is a good universal precedent for the rest of the community.

When you are finished considering these five questions,

you should be well on the way to determining what is the proper course of action FOR YOU. If there are still areas of confusion or doubt, at least you have identified them and can seek further advice and counsel.

Conclusion

As we have seen, the public debate on "suing at the drop of a hat" tends to be distorted by:

1. A remnant of old thought that all litigation is bad;
2. Confusing the two concepts of 'litigiousness';
3. Focusing on torts cases only; and
4. Focusing on 'natural person' litigants only.

Because of this, there is a tendency to assess litigation on the basis of the individual ethics of 'one shotters' rather than seeing it as a structural process influenced by social and economic factors. This is a dangerous mistake to make in a system where as much litigation is initiated by corporations as by natural persons. Indeed, making society less litigious at the behest of corporate 'repeat players' and commercial vested interests may ultimately produce a less harmonious society as individuals lose confidence in the legal system as an agent for the delivery of justice.

In a society adhering to the Rule of Law, citizens have every right to criticize:

- A litigious plaintiff;
- A non-litigious, but otherwise unethical, plaintiff; and

- A law which treats as a 'wrong' something which is not a 'wrong,'

but to go one step further and argue that citizens should be "left in the dark" about their legal rights is incongruous. If the law is wrong, the legislature and/or the courts should adjust it. If the law is right but socially unaffordable, the legislature should say so openly and make the appropriate changes.

Hopefully, this book has introduced you to the jungle out there that is modern litigation and given you some tools to help you navigate your way through it. With clarity of thought, wisdom and courage, you should be able to handle your legal problem in a way that strengthens you as a person. If your decision is not to litigate, you will have learned something about yourself and the things that are truly important to you. If your decision is to litigate, you will know how to conduct yourself with rectitude and how to set a positive example for others.

Good luck!

ABOUT THE AUTHOR

Andrew Thelander worked as a litigation lawyer in Australia for close to ten years. He has a Master of Arts degree in Professional Ethics and Governance and won the Griffith Award for Academic Excellence in 2002. He is a NMAS Nationally Accredited Mediator and Principal of **Grimhala Dispute Resolution Services** based in Brisbane, Australia, a business providing mediation services, conflict coaching and applied legal anthropological research. He is a writer of both fiction and non-fiction books and a blog on litigation ethical issues where your comments and feedback are welcome:

shouldisue.blogspot.com.au

He may be contacted at info@grimhala.com.au

ⁱ *Public Liability Insurance: Analysis for Meeting of Ministers 27 March 2002* (the Trowbridge Report).
ⁱⁱ CT Onions (ed) (1970) *The Shorter Oxford English Dictionary*, Clarendon Press, p. 1153.
ⁱⁱⁱ M Katz, "Mr Lin's Accident Case: A Working Hypothesis on the Oriental Meaning of Face in International Relations and the Grand Scheme" (1969) 78 *Yale Law Journal* 1491.
^{iv} "Knight's Victim Pleads for Tougher Action" *Melbourne Age* 2 October 2002.
^v MWD Rowlands, "Psychiatric and Legal Aspects of Persistent Litigation" (1988) 153 *British Journal of Psychiatry* 317
^{vi} (1974) 9 *Law and Society* 95-160.
^{vii} M Galanter, "Farther Along" (1999) 33 (4) *Law & Society Review* 1113.
^{viii} Engel, DM, "The Oven Bird's Song: Insiders, Outsiders, and Personal Injuries in an American Community" (1984) 18 *Law & Society Review* 551.
^{ix} Australian Law Reform Commission (2000) *Report 89: Managing Justice: A Review of the Federal Civil Justice System*, paragraphs 6.132-6.136.
^x Galanter, M, "Contemporary Legends about the Civil Justice System" (1999) 35
(7) *Trial* 60.
^{xi} CJ DeFrances & SK Smith (1996) *Contract Cases in Large Counties*, Bureau of Justice Statistics.
^{xii} Plato, *The Republic,* translated by B. Jowett, M.A., Book

III
[xiii] *The Nicomachean Ethics of Aristotle*, translated by F H Peters, M.A., 5th edition, Kegan Paul, Trench, Trubner Co, London 1893
[xiv] James Legge, *The Chinese Classics (Confucian Analects)*, Book XII, Chapter XII
[xv] James Legge, *ibid*, Book XIV, Chapter XXXVI
[xvi] James Legge, *ibid*, Book XV, Chapter XVII
[xvii] James Legge, *ibid*, Book XV, Chapter XXVI
[xviii] Bhikkhu Bodhi (trans. Ed.) (2001, 2nd edition) *The Middle Length Discourses of the Buddha*, Wisdom Publications, p. 547
[xix] P Singer (1993) *Practical Ethics*, 2nd edition, Cambridge University Press, p 9.
[xx] Matthew 5:40 (King James version)
[xxi] John Cloney, Chairman of QBE Insurance quoted in the Trowbridge Report (see note 1 above).
[xxii] Insurance Council of Australia, "Public Liability Submission to Ministerial Forum" published at www. ica.com.au/liabilitysub/pressure. asp
[xxiii] For example, see Pavan Sukhdev's book *Corporation 2020*, Island Press, Washington, 2012 and www.corp2020.com
[xxiv] RE Cheit, "Corporate Ambulance Chasers: The Charmed Life of Business Litigation" (1991) *Studies in Law, Politics and Society* 151
[xxv] Law Reform Commission of NSW (1994) *Discussion Paper 36 - Barratry, Maintenance and Champerty*, pp 14-16.